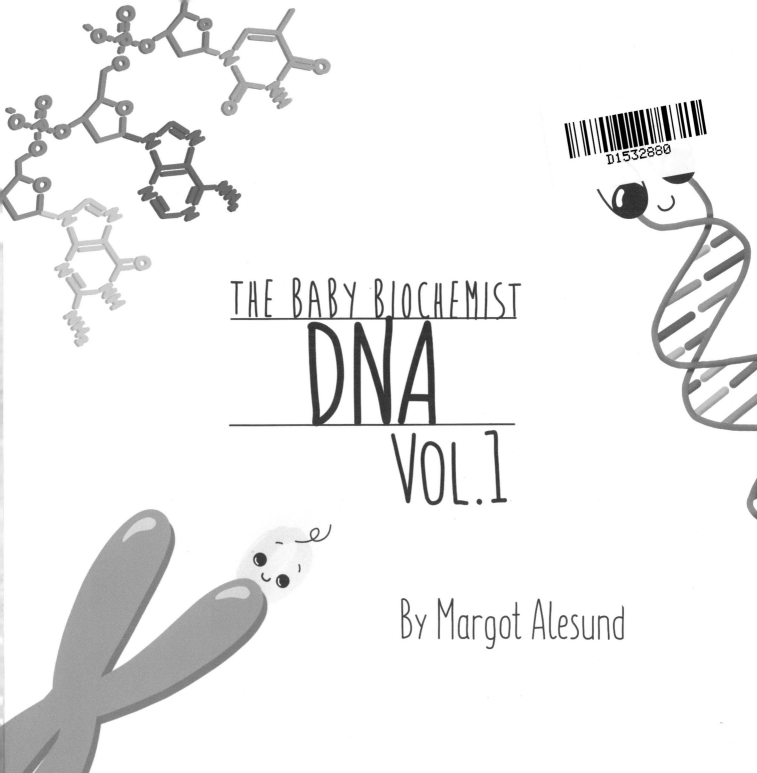

# THE BABY BIOCHEMIST
# DNA
## VOL.1

By Margot Alesund

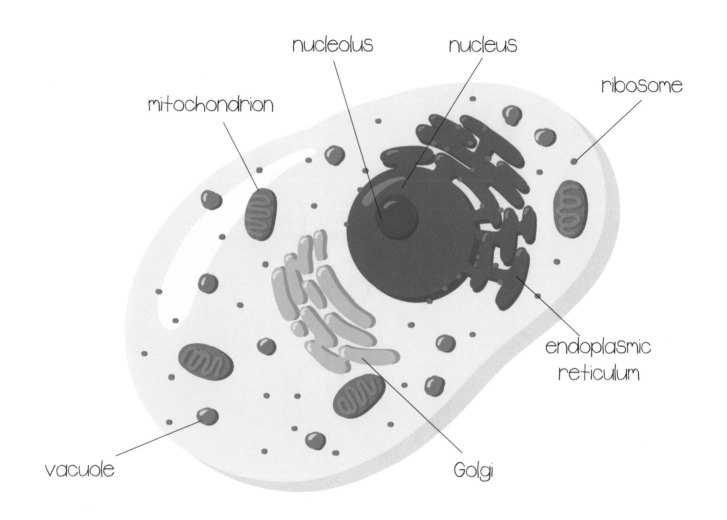

nucleolus

nucleus

ribosome

mitochondrion

endoplasmic
reticulum

vacuole

Golgi

This is a cell.

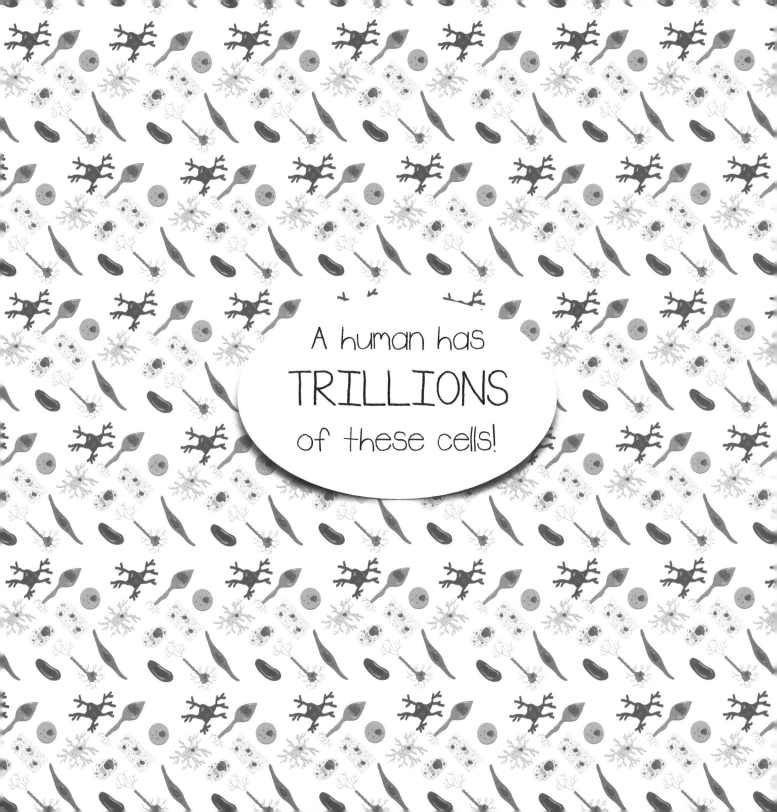

A human has

# TRILLIONS

of these cells!

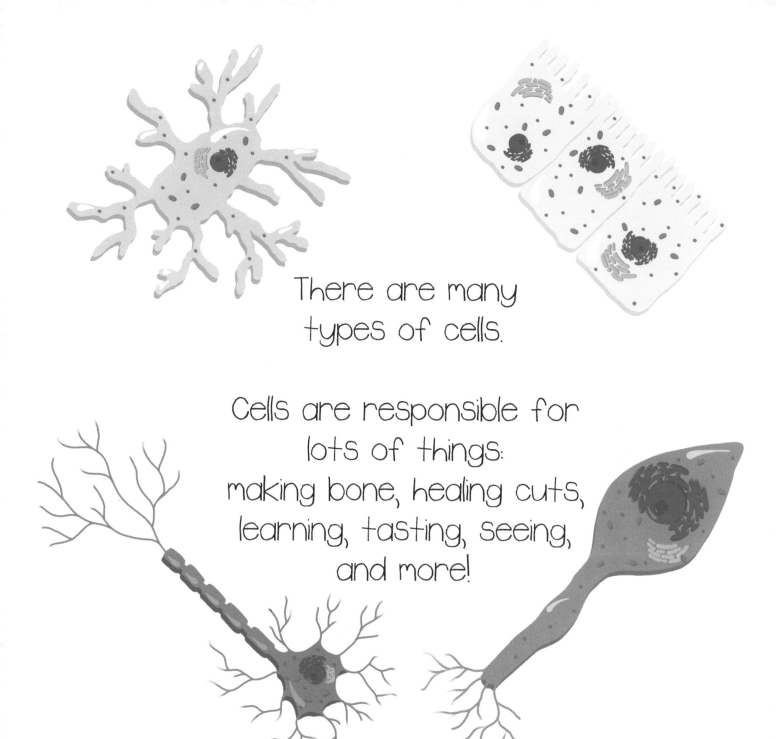

There are many
types of cells.

Cells are responsible for
lots of things:
making bone, healing cuts,
learning, tasting, seeing,
and more!

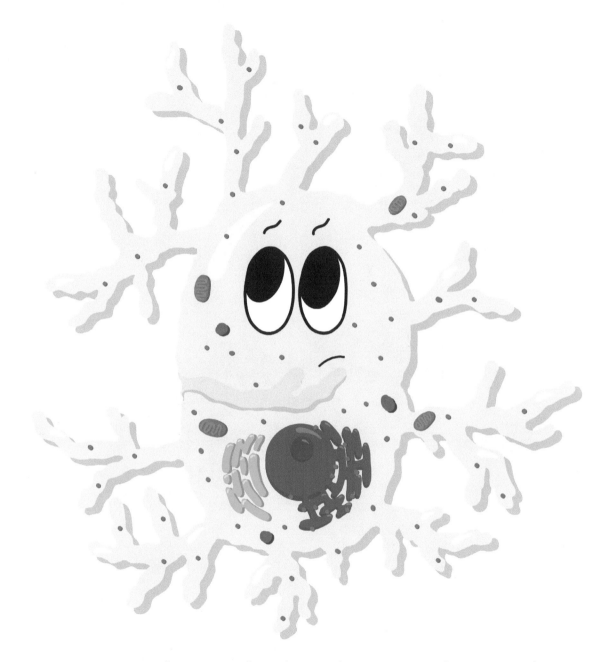

When a cell needs to do something, it needs instructions on how to do it.

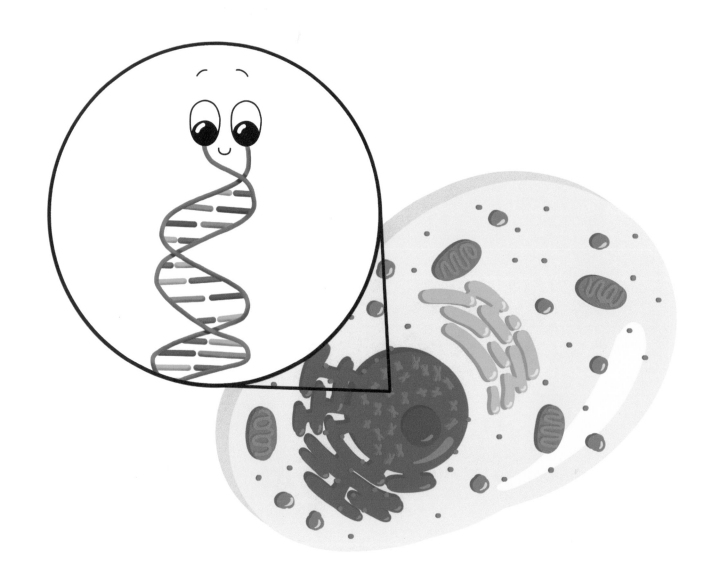

A cell's "instructions" are called DNA and they are stored in the nucleus of the cell.

# DNA is short for deoxyribonucleic acid.

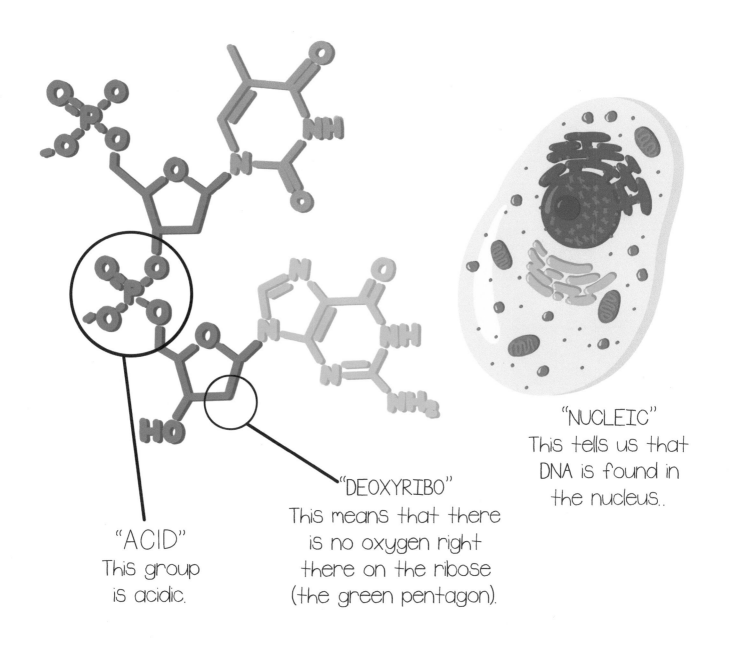

"ACID"
This group
is acidic.

"DEOXYRIBO"
This means that there
is no oxygen right
there on the ribose
(the green pentagon).

"NUCLEIC"
This tells us that
DNA is found in
the nucleus..

DNA is made of four different molecules called NUCLEOTIDES.

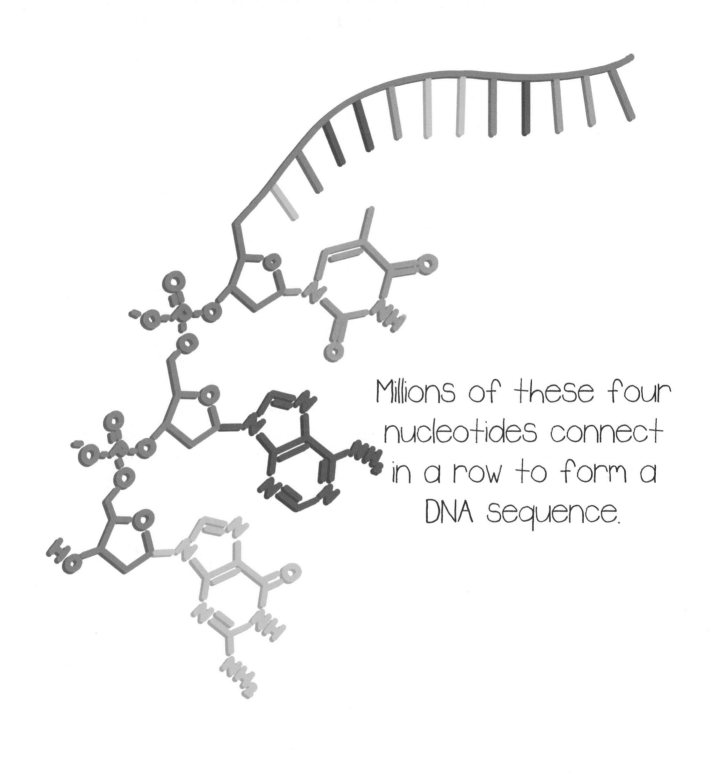

Millions of these four
nucleotides connect
in a row to form a
DNA sequence.

Certain nucleotides can "stick" to
each other, sort of like a magnet
can stick to another magnet.

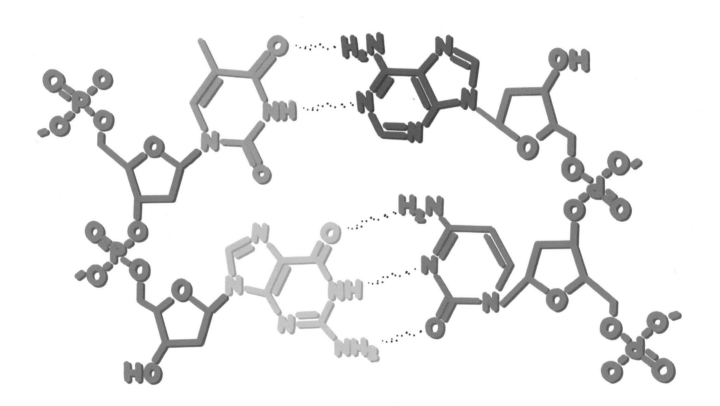

This is called a BASE PAIR.

When the nucleotides on one strand of DNA...

can base pair with another strand...

the two strands stick together!

Because of the shape of the nucleotides, the double stranded DNA curves into something called a DOUBLE HELIX.

The double helix is then wrapped around large molecules called histones.

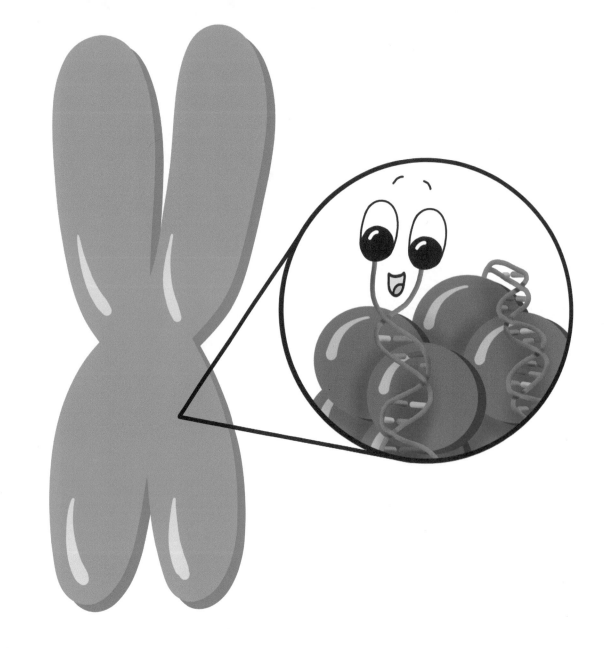

The histones and DNA are gathered
together to form chromosomes.

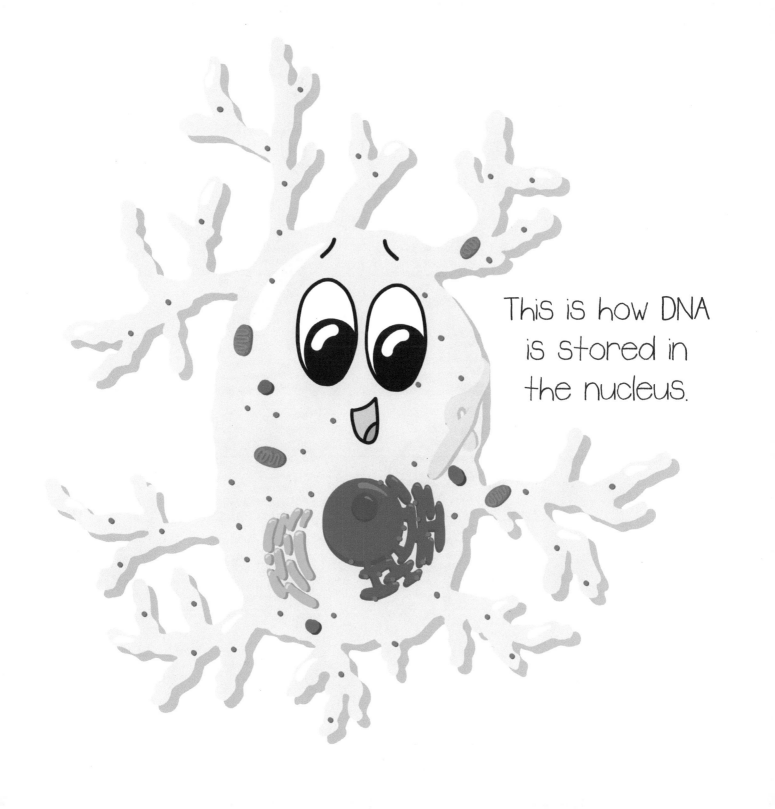

This is how DNA is stored in the nucleus.

The sequence of the DNA is very important.

The cell has lots of ways to fix the
sequence if something damages it.

Some things,
like too much sunlight,
can damage DNA.

When you get a sunburn your cells are telling you, "Hey! Protect your DNA, please!"

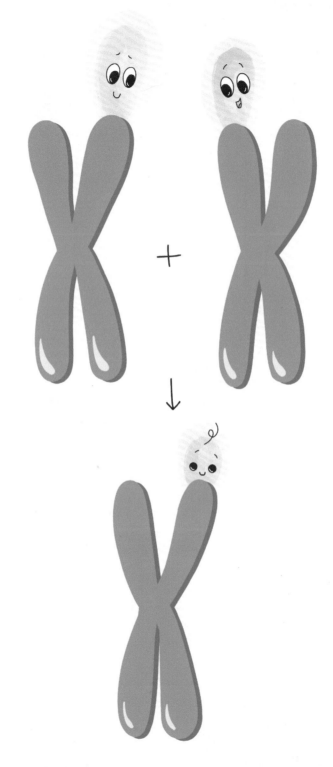

Your parents gave you
your DNA (so keep it safe).

Each of your parents
gave you half of each of
your chromosomes. Wow!

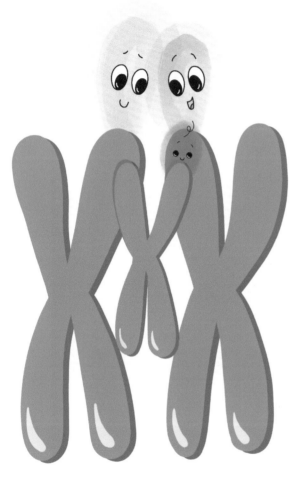

Thanks for my DNA,
parents!

And thanks for telling cells how to work, DNA!

Explore other books in

# THE BABY BIOCHEMIST
series!

## The Baby Biochemist : Proteins

## The Baby Biochemist : RNA

## The Baby Biochemist : Enzymatics

---

Also check out the new series

# BABY MEDICAL SCHOOL

---

All available on Amazon!